Winters Without Snow

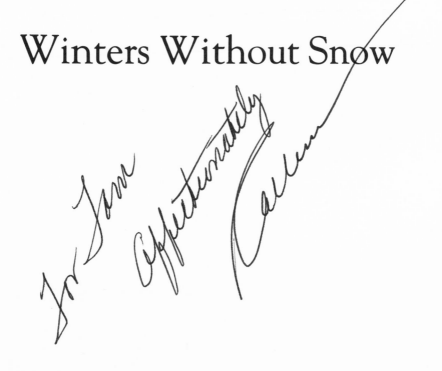

Copyright © 1979 by Colleen J. McElroy
All rights reserved
ISBN #0-918408-17-2
LC # 79-92501
First Printing
Printed in the United States of America

This project was supported by grants from the National Endowment
for the Arts and the New York Council of the Arts.

Book Design by Andrea DuFlon
Cover drawing by Peter Urio
Back cover photo by Michael E. Bry

I. Reed Books is a division of Reed & Cannon. Main office: 285 East
3rd St., New York City, N.Y. 10009. Order Department: I. Reed
Books, 2140 Shattuck Ave., Rm. 311, Berkeley, CA 94704.

ACKNOWLEDGMENTS

Grateful acknowledgment is extended to the following publications for permission to reprint the following poems: *Aphra* (spring 1975), for "Master of the Blue Mask"; *Aspen Anthology*, No. 1 (1976), for "How to Become a Mistress"; *Black Warrior Review* (spring 1976), for "To Whom Do You Wish To Speak"; *Black World* (November 1975), for "The Silence"; *The Chowder Review* No 9 (1977), for "Breaking the Kula Ring"; *Essence* (March 1972), for "loneliness for Nona"; *Essence* (March 1975), for "Day Help"; *Fragments* (Winter 1974), for "U Turn in MoClips"; *Fragments* (Spring 1975), for "Reasons for Poetry"; *Mill Mountain Review* No 2 (1975), for "And They Said It Would End in Fire" and "To My Audience"; *Nimrod* 21, No. 1/2 (1977), for "A Poem For My Old Age"; *Out of Sight* No 3 (1974), for "Indulgence" and "After You've Seen Kansas"; *Poetry Northwest* 17, No. 2 (1976), for "Memoirs of American Speech: Stimulus Response"; *Raindance* 1, No. 1 (1977), for "Questions to a Gypsy Woman"; *Sunbury—a poetry magazine* (Winter 1974), for "Liberation"; *13th Moon* 2, No. 1 (1974), for "Inside the City"; *13th Moon* 2, No. 2 and 3, No. 1 (1975), for "Pedestrians"; *Willow Springs* 1, No 1 (1977), for "Out Here Even Crows Commit Suicide"; *Xanadu* No 4 (1977), for "Memoirs of American Speech: From the Womb to the Tomb" and "There Are No Absolutes"; *Yardbird Reader*, for "The Griots Who Knew Brer Fox"; *The Pushcart Prize: Best of the Small Presses* (edited by Bill Henderson, New York: The Pushcart Press, 1976), for "The Griots Who Knew Brer Fox"; *The Third Woman: Minority Women Writers of the United States* (edited by Dexter Fisher, Boston: Houghton Mifflin, 1980), for "Dancing With the Fifth Horseman (Living Under the Wing: Part 2)" and "Defining It For Vanessa."

for Vanessa and Kevin

TABLE OF CONTENTS

I

Liberation

I breathe from the stomach to ease the pain,
No one wets a finger to touch my wound.
My heart pumps so loud, I hear my own echo
But sound cannot plug the wound.
I gulp and sunlight hurts. It expects
A dry gulch, finds instead a field of weeds
And wet moss, my chest the fungus bearer,
My tears draining into its sewage.

I learn to feed the wound.
Already I've forgotten Ishtar's ancient chants,
Believe the universe is temporary.
I bury myself in fantastic fabrics
And wait for each climax of pain.
Yesterday, I heard the buzz saw
Of developers cut into my left ventricle
Aiming for the open space behind my eyelids.
They have already surveyed my vulva
For a new high rise, culled and simplified
My passions. The blade hits center,
The wound is finally free.
And my blood erupts deep red and infectious.
They are repulsed. It is too thick, too rich.
It is too female.

Memoirs of American Speech

I.
From the Womb to the Tomb

you will learn to speak
just repeat after me
please
      thank you
           hello
your arms will move in 80′ arcs
your tongue will click
without drooling
you will identify ships
in the harbor
   say it
       S.S. Ulysses
             Ticonderoga
  now
        slowly
you will know the meaning of color
  green grass
        good
true blue
        fine
black night
       red blood
stop
   it's not your turn
raise your hand only if you hear
the sound
pay attention
move your head with your hands
try this
   MyFathersaysbaNanaNanaoil
don't stammer
        speak slowly

follow me
       you will need this
inhale   exhale
          watch closely
               count this
one thousand bars in this block
one hundred whores
you must make decisions
you must cast a shadow
let's say it together
     the policeman is my friend
the city's too pretty for death
this is a circle
          this is a square
these blocks are all the same
speak clearly
         listen closely
once more
      after me
the baby is normal
            normai

II.
Voice Print

In the dark womb sacs of your
lungs,
Les Fleurs du Mal grow
like mushrooms
on the dank floor
of a barn.
Your chest blooms grey
in a sunset
of x-ray shadows
like sagebrush
fertilized by nicotine.
In the final scene
you are the star;
death by inhalation
but not yet dead
enough
to crumble exquisitely
into a Hollywood faint.
You know the cause
having Bogarted your own role
like some gangster's moll,
cigarette dangling
from your lips
to prove you're wise and sexy.
From the first puff to the last
that sweet, sweet taste
graces the tip of your tongue,
floats seductively
to the edge of your teeth
before tumbling pell-mell
down your throat;
a landslide against canyon walls
carrying wafer thin flesh.

Echoes of that slide
ascend later
in the shrill pierce of a wheeze
or thundering cough.
The flowers dig in,
the silt crowds upward
for air
and each breath becomes
a small failure.

III.
Post-operative

You were out of place, George
Catering to a Wall Street crowd
In a back alley town; explaining
Yourself with weather reports;
Howling the midnight news
Over the local radio station
As if it were important by the time
It reached that town.
Your blonde hair didn't fit
The heart that ached behind
Background music, notes
To friends about drink-ins, orgies.
You separated truth; glueing
Your face to that mike, your wink
Causing static in the station's
Main line. What happened?
Did you go mad watching
The spinning discs and clocks
In twelve hour sets; holding down
A violent urge to hurl batting
Scores, stock averages against
The walls? Did spirits come in
Fighting over the part of you
That wanted to be fat; spectral
Forms haunting your soul,
The part that was black? Surgeons
Scored your heart, now the market's
Dropped; the number two clamp
Set tight in your chest plugged
Your brain. Some insane fool
Has your mike, soothing the world
With music and facts.
The daily grind took up the slack
Your heart left bare.

IV.
Homunculus
        (for Daddy Glip)

I wanted to take you home
tired old man
do small favors to put smiles
on your wrinkled face
that graph of liquor sales
and failures
lines for too many jobs
left unfinished
too many women left
somewhere with maybe
another son

I wanted you around
in place of my own grandpa
whose memory had grown
too small to fill
my son's days
I forgot this was a new age
where old age
doesn't fit
noisy rooms and small children

we're afraid these days
of warping young minds
with the honesty of death
afraid your stories
will make the programmed
future seem small
I almost forgot
old men are built
for rest

those massive hands
of yours that shake
have to grow brittle
and still
you are needed to fill space
in places built for languishing
until death
your arms must hold needles
and you must embarrass
sheets and nurses

I forgot that once
you graduate from life
you make your home
among the rest of the aging
or die after three years
asleep in the back
of the family house
in its smallest room

V.
No Words Are Necessary

her husband beats her
he's thin as twine
his glands dried
from mustard gas
      aftermath
of a pimps and pushers war
he says she's country
but she won't speak

it must be subdural
her sentences clogged
from too much fatback
and beans
dry bread and butter
put her on a diet
drain the fat into tubes
stew out the juice

still no words
open the skull
rattle the cerebellum
crack it like a clam's shell
and pour in the nouns
the verbs will follow later
still grunts you say
she's too benign
her spine must leap and snap
each vertebra become
perfect as fresh new peas
submerge the torso
in heated baths
apply glycerine above the neck

electrodes please
the knife and the needles
find the switch   turn
the shock to full volume
trace the missing plurals
the system must respond

what   no answer   linguistically
impossible   code the dialect
plug in the computer
46, pregnant, mute and black
          we have no name
for this kettle of fish
toss her in the alley out back
mark no refund
on the welfare check

VI.
Stimulus-Response

when flames dressed the music store
in a gaudy cabaret of colors and smoke
I thought of news reports   night riders
bats and dancing bigots   how panic needs
the courage of sound   the hero's scream
before the charge   the fear of silent men
I remembered speechless children
the hours of painful sibilants
piercing narrow clinic rooms
remembered how I hissed   sharp and direct
between perfectly articulated teeth

I listened for guitars singing in the blaze
their strings stretching and popping
like petals of deadly red flowers
piano strings twanging in chorus
harmonicas screaming toward the melody
the wind drafts add riffs   but I cannot hear
I am glued to the sibilant crowd
we grind our teeth on the acrid air

we are drawn to the fire   awed
as any Neanderthal   its primal sounds
triggering our ancient ears   a signal
confusing the magic of words   reminding us
that death is the absence of sound
entranced by the flames
we are dumb as deaf mutes   tomorrow
we'll play with coughs and grunts
groping for speech
understanding less and less

loneliness for Nona

Black woman lost
in hot cat eyes
smoky, sweaty skin
fog rising
from the pores
as coffle chains clank
in a hazy cloak
arms shovel
deep into the wet
mud of some
empty battlefield
slave bones
rattle in the damp
cellar of a coastal castle
washed by Africa's sea
the sound screams
toward the porch
where you sit
rattling ice
in your glass of scotch
and you search
for your husband's tears
formed in a white man's war
and lost
on this city's streets

Running Out of Time
(for Diana Sands 1934-73)

thirty-nine
and at your peak
pushing for time
to turn pages in a book
without fumbling
time to rewrite
misspelled words
or leisurely listen to nonsense songs

you stretch seconds into minutes
mastering artistic tricks
glowing for every
black woman in your audience
wait patiently
through someone else's gripe
your own pain clutches the throat

a race against time
fitting lines in between busses and green lights
you are quoted
        Diana on location in Lebanon
        Diana blending color
        into starring roles
        Shakespeare, St. Joan, Georgia
        Georgia, Georgia, Hello Mother
Diana's phone voice recorded
the fantasy of films becomes home

occasionally you become
acutely aware of differences
the smell of sun and oil   colors
but later find it's unimportant
there are too many trumpets
fine wines   sunsets and seascapes
they hardly know you here
vaguely remember your name
off some cheap marquee

there are too few days
to use your footsteps
as a measure of your existence
you pace your duration
by the spread of blotches
between the breasts
the scalpel
fails to stop
the rampant growth of tissue

nerves shoot curious
impulses to the skin's surface
you fail to understand them

you are female and famous
untouched by the natural
order of things
you bathe in holy water
at Lourdes
coolly drinking its sweet wetness
your blackness adding depth
to its meaning

in the final cycle of minutes
your brain begs for sleep
footlights   friends
and celluloid loves fade
as you face the final fear
the unknown color
of limitless time

Concrete Things Like Sections of an Orange
(for Kevin)

you leave at dusk
eating dirt for miles
you are heading west
you will see the dusty outskirts
of too many towns
you will cry for years
soaking in distant sunsets
and strange skylines
your blackness will glow
like precious sea coral

you are travelling
from nowhere
to this place
everyone follows with envious looks
even pirates wave forlornly
at your retreating shadow
you are travelling
with poets
you find delight in the surprise
of small things like chambers
of the heart, shiny rocks
sections of an orange

you tint your windows green
swing from rust to grey
never naming the colors
glide into currents
like some Yangtze peddler
travelling west by east
on a fuzzy map of fading light
you pick up bits and pieces
of someone else's dreams
carry rain in umbrellas
enchant and mystify
with fingerholes of wonder

you fascinate and confuse
those who would cut the world
into line plots and grave stones
far behind is family
far behind friends
who fail to capture beauty
in the silence of watching
above there's the swept wings
of single birds
in front the ocean roaring
even when no one is listening

Reasons for Poetry

I let poems
bend my life
like a Möbius strip,
each image
rotates today
into tomorrow
in flat 180
degree arcs.
I get high on poetry,
let a line
take me beyond
the next mountain range
where my stanzas
glitter like fragments
of a broken mirror.
I hold the sharp edges
of white paper
against my black flesh
and like the last
of the devil dancers,
I feed the verse
till it dies.
And when you have
eaten me
down to my fingertips,
I put a poem
on my pillow
use its words
like a dildo;
then like the sky,
I have no place to go
but up.

Enter My Head

Fresh roasted fingers
From too much smoke,
Pale purple moons on my thumbnails
Must seem like earthrise
To the microbes crawling in the dark
Cracks and bends of my hands.

The screams inside my head
Are by-lines, rhythmed phrases,
Essence of plot
For some sad story
In a small town journal.
That sound keeps me awake.

Symphonic red eyelids
With trumpet bursts of carousel white
Flash treble, flash trouble.
Hospital green skull
Where the intern makes his rounds
With a blind man's stylus.

This sweet gas smell
Ringing agony that begs answers.
Heaps of newspaper words
Stacked in some forgotten corner
Of my brain,
Holds mildew stains like piss rings,
Hold my answers fuzzy.

I walk numb, ears bundled
In surgeon's boots poke oddly out.
Gulping gill-fed air
Trading fin for foot;
Spawn only in season
Thinking of friends I've had.

The nurse fills my cheeks
In mute chartreuse.
Equipped for family hour,
Tubes are tied for comfort.
I watch anarchists
In scheduled press conferences.
Attend hem line wars.

Drop by cloudly drop,
Blood plasma claims my fears.
I am swallowed in identifying numbers.
Concrete pillars of freeway feeder
Lines rest beyond my vision;
Shiny chrome of recycled revolutions.
Lies my lovers told me.
Licorice women grown bitter.

They use the knife,
Smiling like talk show hosts.
Separate instinct from success;
Hoping I will recover,
Learn to laugh, sing
And breathe subaqueous air.

II

Winters Without Snow

Under the grey smother of clouds,
The layers of grey upon grey,
Mist rolls against earth
Like unwound spools of ribbon
For a shroud.   The rotting stumps
Of an abandoned dock are glued to the sky.
Ships cling to the fringe like bits of lace.
There is no earth.

Under the constant drizzle, plastic arches
And pale neon letters pulse like muffled
Heartbeats.   Even brick and stone fade.
Only monoliths of Federal, Bank and Insurance
Seem real.   Under the soft wet grey,
The only signs of life are the swish of rubber
As tires cut across wet pavement.
The leaves are grey.

The land, the water
Even your hair is grey.   Light clogs your chest
And your moans echo hollow against the mushy air.
You turn inward, broiling against thunderheads
That never come to full steam.   Picking absently
At fungus on your brow, you try bringing your hand
Into focus, remembering how it felt to turn warm fingers
This way and that.

After You've Seen Kansas

After you've seen Alaska,
every place looks like Kansas . . .

in the gold curtains
covering my view of the mountains
shadows of Kansas flow
even here among the mountains
I see ocean waves of wheat
the wild places where weeds
dry and roll into filigree balls
swirling across the flat land
like some lost feather
from a handsome Indian
who sat too well on his pinto

each dawn the land nods and folds back
from the lamp black thickness of night
the wind sighs sending whistle thin notes
through reed thin wheat grass
the sound moves swiftly
pacing the troubled land
like a cat's padded feet
the dust brushes against your cheeks
fine grains buffing away sharp edges
the air is wet is hot

the land is flat
and you are warm near the soil
it is not the cold distance that's here
the lonely strange mountains
that demand your eye
in the Kansas sun
I was earth black and lava
caught on a flat sky line
of red dunes and lemon grass
the expanse of sky and ground
rolled out like a map
miles of flat bronze where sky and earth
triangled end upon end

at night the sound of mad winds
shrill as hooded riders pierced the stillness
I could expand become sand and katydid
or soar like a black winged bird
above corn and sunflower rows
tall as sharecropper's huts
I could ride through towns clustered
like bandits along the Big Blue and Smokey rivers
I could call to the moon hanging round and orange
on the shallow plate of a sage yellow horizon

here I have swallowed tatters
of a shattered moon
here the mountains are green
the sky is a cold grey sea
and I wheeze among green
when I'm dry I look for friends
long to pull the sun into cycles
of lean days and nights
I follow the moon but she is cold
and can not bear to sleep
without a lover

The Griots Who Know Brer Fox

There are old drunks among the tenements,
old men who have been
                     lost
forever from families, shopping centers
starched shirts and
                  birthdays.
They are the griots, the story tellers
whose faces are knotted and swollen
         into a black patchwork
         of open sores and
         old scabs; disease
         transforms the nose
         into cabbage   the eyes
         are dried egg yolks.
They grind old tobacco between scabby gums
like ancient scarabs rolling dung from tombs
in their
                  mother country.
In this country, they are scenic, part of the
view from Route 1, Old Town.

Don't miss them; they sit in doorways
of boarded houses in the part of town
nestled between wide roads named for
English kings and tourists.
         These old men sit like moldy stumps
         among the broken bricks of narrow
         carriage streets, streets paved
         with the Spirits of '76,
         the Westward Movement and Oz.

These old men never travel the wide roads;
they sit in the dusk, dark skinned as Aesop,
remember their youth. They chant stories
to keep themselves awake another day;
        tales of girls bathing in kitchens
        before wood stoves, smells of
                the old South.
        Or Northern tales of babies bitten
        by rats, women who've left them
        or how they were once rich.
They'll spin a new Brer Rabbit story for a nickel;
tell you how he slipped past the whistle-slick fox
to become
        the Abomey king.
But you must listen closely,
it moves fast, their story
skipping and jumping childlike;
the moral hidden in an enchanted forest
            of word games.
        These stories are priceless,
        prized by movie moguls
        who dream of Saturday matinees
        and full houses.
You have to look beyond the old men's faces,
beyond the rat that waits to nibble the hand
when they sleep. The face is anonymous,
              you can find it anywhere
but the words are as prized
as the curved tusks of the bull elephant.

Illusion

I hate wide mouth black girls
with their loud walnut faces.
I hate their bright white eyes
and evil tongues,

their hen cackle laughs
that startle birds
roosting in trees miles away.
I hate their graceful jungle steps,
the steps they fall into too easily,
a downbeat only they can hear .

They stir cities,
cause concrete to tremble.
I hate the way their backs
taper into a narrow base
before spreading, graceful
round and proud as a peacock's.

Their firm black legs
insult me with swift movements,
feet in tempo even as they walk
to pick up the evening paper;
turning pages noisily to find
comic strips, the rustle of paper
paced with the pop of many sticks
of Juicy Fruit.

I hate the popping fingers,
the soft flash of color
turning like butterscotch buds
in a field of wind wild
dandelion greens.

I turn away from high cheek bones
and wide spread mocha nostrils
finely honed to catch the scent
of paddy-rollers or pig faced sheriffs.

This country has made them
sassyfaced.
They sneer at mousey mongoloid blondes
who move coolly blind
through a forest of suburbs,
lisping about posh uptown hotels.

I hate the pain that makes them
bulldog their way through
downtown crowds,
makes them nurture dead minds
and naturally accent cheap clothes
with finely curved licorice colored shoulders.

They bury Nefertiti charms
under outstretched lips,
grow older under frowns
and a hurricane of bad manners;

they grow barbed, cold,
these Sapphires and Mabel Sues
from ebony to dusky brown,
from creme and rust to lemon yellow.

They are my sisters
and we sit in a barracks of noise,
trading screams with wandering
no-caring   louder   brothers.

Day Help

She's fat
  each wrinkle
  marks a new frustration
  a fine wine she didn't drink
  the fur coat she caressed
  in another woman's closet.
  Her hands are the color
  of fertile earth
  and can't type without error
  despite the six month course

She took
  four years ago—
  courtesy, equal opportunity.
  Her upper arms hang loose
  keep her warm
  covering the once firm
  muskmelon breasts
  that now hang
  like fudge melting.
  The underside of her elbows
  smells of rose water
  and glycerine.

She answers
to her first name.
Her hair smells of cabbage,
her face is full
eyes cautious
even when she tells a joke.
Kitchens, broom closets
and dust rags are not in her dreams.
White folks who call her
'our gal Mae'
never see her slim
in an office suit
or crisp as lettuce
in a cashmere coat
without those wide hips
and ankles that swell
with each winter.

Master of the Blue Mask

In the fish store
the tetras swim
through blue haze water.
A bulbous worm
called fish
wafts like a falling leaf
through plastic fern.
His flat cousin pleats
through amazon sword
and hair grass.
Packages of fern
line one wall
and are labeled "living
ocean."
Next door a shiny disc
defies the edges of his tank.
He's round and yellow
like a slice of cheddar cheese
with fins.
His mouth is drawn and mean.
His bottom sawblades
through machine aired water.
He is masked in blue.
The lone ranger of his own world.

I feel his eyes searching
the universe
under that mask.
I want to peel away the blue.
He circles, bumps the glass pane
then trots off with quick
shark strokes
toward lower reaches
of fake coral
before turning to attack again.
The fish store seller is tanned.
He is keeper
of the lone ranger.
His smile is mysterious
and he soothes me with tales
of salt and fresh water beauties.
His eyes twinkle like pebbles
from a distant Pacific beach.
I leave the store
walk out in the wet Seattle world
to swim among the unkind crowds.
I imagine myself
master of the blue mask.

Inside the City

the world is housed in glass
it sucks
        you in with noise
                its sap
        makes you jumpy
                the machine oil
                the circuit breakers
make you turn down gifts, hate babies
        think seriously about burning books
you sleep hungry, eat tired and bitter
you eat
                city living
grinding indigestion between your teeth
along with broken mufflers, motorcycles and trucks
cars grind up the hill
your living room
                their race track
they roar like the last charge
before a screaming troop of foot soldiers
        they are manned
                by bored housewives
who take their anger out in pistons
driving
        fat no necked children
                to endless lessons
husbands squeal around corners
        racing toward new lovers
                more dead hours
a clanking furnace is background noise
your living room
                throbs
        the tv is cadence
        you're the time bomb
even the con man car salesman
works with the rhythm, looking for suckers
                for you

his sales pitch insistent
>louder than the ever pregnant
>soap opera's lines
the music box your daughter bought
to soothe your nerves
>is tympany
you're never sure the drama's trapped
inside the tube
>you're bitchy
>>modern
>and can't trust anyone
you sleep to escape
the noise is in your dreams, sharp
>steel grey and thin
>>you stumble
>falling dead center
>on the knife

U Turn in MoClips

You can step into Georgia out there,
Step back in time
Or remember the stink
Of some rabbit town up North.
Indians eat nuggets
Under gas flares,
Dishwater whites shake clams
From their hip boots.
Old shadows roost in pigeon lofts
On the county school roof.
There is no time here.

The grey rotting line
Of makeshift cabins
Is cut by the bright pink
Cottage of the town's widow
Like a distress signal.
There is nothing here for me.
Nothing to feed my blackness.
The wind is westerly
And the fragile line of timber
Treasures its eastern coat
Of leaves.
The antique shop is empty.

Only the gulls see it.
Those who live here
Are short as scrub pine
And never look up.
Fine lines make them quaint.
The town dies slowly
Like an old woman;
First, the stomach goes,
Then the eyes.

There are no trains in MoClips.
A truck rots in the spawning
Stream,
Its clock stopped.
The sun is cold.
And the ocean is bigger than
Summer.

Pedestrian

they are like stone age fish
these feet
black, thorny and primitive
as trilobites
bones and joints are jammed
in sublaxation
they have seen too many concrete stairs
and carpeted prisons
they ache for African beaches
cone crowned and oaken
their supports have failed
the arches
always shallow
now rest ground-level flat
they are in ruins
and show no knowledge of place names
or regular pressure points
they lack dorsal flexion
and adequate range of motion
calloused, bruised
and tossed on too many ancient currents
they refuse to dance
or take advantage of sunlight

The Myth Makers
(for John Gardner)

you are like a book
of vivid Welsh dreams
singleminded as Benin kings
who believed in the sheer power
of personal blood

even your slight paunch
suggests feasts
in cold castles
your smile
uneven as a rosary of charms
worn by Druids

your myths echo the lines
etched and grouped in your hands
like characters from Gothic plays
you move on gusts of wind
uneasy murmurs of air
from caves, bogs or hoarfrost

you break codes
of consonantal languages
plead innocence
in the wake of confusion
as you flee toward fogbound moors
your eyes like astroblue stones
plucked from space

you focus on distant points
conjure and shape our lives
we dance to charm you
and we are charmed
you draw us into stories of horror
feed us scraps of fascination.

toss us tales spun through your hair
like rings from the moon
beckon us to fall through
layers of light
and like gaunt hounds
we drool and beg
for blood and bones

And They Said It Would End in Fire

it all began with a mechanic
who succumbed to an oversexed engine
became so devoted, he worshipped it
    as a living thing, carried it everywhere
    on a red velvet pillow
one day he turned his back
and was sucked into the exhaust
of a compact
    a loud but ravenous model
then helicopters, lawn mowers
mini-bikes joined in
    a full cycle evolution
    the earth spinning
    its poles drawing pistons
    and cylinders together
cats and birds were easily devoured
cars blossomed into deadly ferns
    spinning their runners across pavement
    concrete slabs cracked and new stalks
    were formed
    tentacles intertwined, some hanging
    from what had once been bridges
    sucking in pedestrians and
    crunching them like popcorn
the breath was sucked from babies
virgins were pulled from cloisters by creeping
vines, their nun's habits ripped
from their bodies
    pimps were salted and chewed
    by their gleaming chariots
    windows of those deuce-and-a-quarters
    glowing greenly before transformation

large white-on-white-in-whites
ate only non-whites
keeping within worldly customs
demure professorial sedans attacked librarians
while pink convertibles waited for juicy
debutantes and tanks found a good
supply of die-hard veterans
      skyscrapers were jet driven
      into the pulsating green of prickly leaves
      stalks oozed their way through
state offices, munching traffic citations
books of law enforcing speed limits
patrolmen, silver badges and all
      speed demons and gas mongers
      were saved for last
      their aperitifs
      were motorcycles blended with their riders
after the first rain
petals of oddly shaped flowers
licked the last bit
of axle grease
      and the planet moved
      gracefully, silently around its sun

III

Living Under the Wing

1.
Sometimes you awake
In the hollows of predawn dark.
Your room has changed its shape,
Claims shadows of strange proportions,
Doors and windows don't exist.

Some days the sun is an aluminum
Disc shining behind a blanket of fog,
Glowing like the blind eye
Of some alien planet.

There are days when the wind
Seeks the sea only to die on the rocks
Of some ancient coastline
And your appeals to Nereid
Are lost in the currents.

Hours are lost waiting by a telephone
That is silent as death,
While you are caught
Between your horoscope
And the weather.

When the screeching voice
Of someone else's wife,
Thin and shrill as strung cat gut
Floods you with bad memories
Of yourself.

When loneliness traps your ovaries
In twin rings of pain.
When you want to be lovingly tender,
But find yourself trapped in a scream
That will linger
Months after your death.

These are the days when your targets
Are all wrong and your timing is off.
When you are like a plane
That goes mushy and noses in, belly up.
When diving through air
Or into the sea,
You are still the same.

2.

"If you drape 39 iron chains over your
arms and do a dance, the whole point
of the dance will be to seem light and
effortless."

—Robert Francis

One day, you stepped
Into my horoscope
Bringing summer
And a view of the mountains
I had never known
You insisted on answers
I said for better or worse
Not knowing your definition
Of time and closing distance
In the singular sky
Of my dreams
I tried to fly tandem
Your wingtip to mine

Last summer you left
My life quivering
Like a battlefield
I wore headaches like garments
You cut me so thin
My lunar cycle was left
Without a channel
I angrily snatched the next
Egg from its bloody cradle
Now, veins show
Where I have no veins
And age hangs
Flat against my face
Still, I don't know
How to answer my anger

I tear myself dry
With memories
The sky fills
With your shadows
A rain heavy cloud
The feathered cry
Of north bound geese
I hear Mama's complaints
Louder than your vows
But I know you are there
I find your scribbled notes
You dreamed of brisk mountains
Desert air and Ponce de Leon girls
I saw myself
In your lunar dreams
Trapped in a strange language
Under a muggy mooned sky

Now, I drape myself
In slammed doors, confused answers
And friends as definite
As the wind or shadows
My friends slice the moon
And sprinkle the night
Around my ears
They cut me even thinner
I don't believe in them
But find little else I can trust

You practiced your dreams
Running against traffic
Racing home sweaty and happy
Falling across the bed
Like a surf pushing against
My excuses
Of work, motherhood, blackness
And a world I know too well

I was thirty-nine today
And the air repeats
He is gone, he is gone
All day I swayed to its chant
But have not yet learned
To move with the rhythm
Tonight I fell
Into the pit of my pillow
Fighting dreams rising around me
Like clouds of perfume
I am caught in a symphony of years
My pulse racing with each crescendo
When exhaustion becomes
The silver bullet
Plunging me into timeless sleep
I race away from you
Into the moon
Laughing with relief
Light headed with the pleasure
Of definite speed.

3.
This is what it is all about
The thin cord of pain
Like a sliver of cloud caught
On the leading edge of a jet's wing

It is a lonely goat
Leaping from cliff to ledge
In search of sweet lichen

It is the lining of my stomach
Silver and heavy as we fly low
Over the silent moon-scaped ice cap

It is the stillness as we undress
Waiting for sudden shifts of air
That will suck us into love

Or how I watch you stroke and check
The dials of a float plane
How the right mix of fuel excites your fingers

It is the ghosts that walk
The ice cap, the cold reef
We fly above with lonely eyes

The shadow of wings
Across a rookery, myopia
Softening my view of mountains

Or a muddy patch of water laced muskeg
It is how islands rise up like breasts
Perfect in their irregular curves

It is how we finally learn
To avoid the shadows
Avoid the oneness with a new kiss

It is my fear of love
My need to leave yet stay
It is the myth of angel's wings

Darkness and evil witches
The indefinite shadow of death
That flies across this planet

It is what we have become
This living under the wing

Questions to a Gypsy Woman

how do you go there with all
your crocks and kettles
your poems and superstitions?
I have surrounded myself
with bric-a-brac
strangers, husbands, friends
like old books full of myths
in my rooms
crimes pay
the good guys are black
the princess gets drunk
slaughters prince charming
and his white horse
I share these tales with ghosts
they feed me fattening foods
spiked with cholesterol
tars and nicotine
they love my cluttered rooms

how will your children grow
running this way and that
with no ties and no wealth?
the mind is a cluttered room
forced by the body's juices
to snap and crackle
on invisible electric wires
threads of the real and unreal
notice how I've imagined you
pulled you from wishful
years of debris
piece by romantic piece
one blink and you're discarded
draped with the veil of yesterdays
like sagging sofas and chairs
filling corners of useless rooms.

if you lift the covers of the mind
clutter will tumble and scatter
like puppies playing in the sand
or barn swallows in May
once they're out
it's up to you
you can sort them like junk mail
decks of cards
lovers
or you can abandon yourself
in varicolored dreams
and like a poet
reshape reality

Villanelle for Madness

Lady, your mind is turned raw side out
Watching dragons eat your birthday cake
Dropping penny arcade soldiers with one shot

Doctor, doctor, watch her slowly nibble suicide
A negative color packages her in a world of false pride
Lady, your mind is turned raw side out

An aging black sex trick; astrologically deep, yet lame
Sucked efficiently into an old fun house game
Watching dragons eat your birthday cake

Each candle is a man you wanted but lost
Those wet dreams that kept your reality in check
Dropping penny arcade soldiers with one shot

Fantasy is fake bat wings glued to success
You played to the hilt, snarling when you were hot
But lady, your mind is turned raw side out

Mama, your wisdom was not mother earth, not sweet
Just added guilt spots to the black lady's dream sheets
And she ages watching dragons eat her birthday cake

Full grown seeds from her black womb strike her paranoia hot
Ain't it alive, ain't it love, men are true, ain't it life
Lady, your mind is turned raw side out
Dropping penny arcade soldiers with one shot

Out Here Even Crows Commit Suicide

In a world where all the heroes
are pilots with voices like God
he brought her a strand of some woman's

hair to wear on her wing.
She looked sideways at the ground
silent behind the cloudy film covering

her eyes knowing she would be his
forever. They cruised the city nights
each one spiralling away from the other

but always coming home to gather stories.
Dark streets bright tavern lights drunks
filled with beer in the gutters.

The flicker of stars shaped like a hunter's
arrow bent stars that twinkled like babies'
eyes. No babies for them. She was an outcast.

He a loner. A perfect pair.
Winters had made him wise
And he avoided the single nests of summer.

He told her about things she could see
How the dismal cover of clouds roil and explode
and the ground aches like an old woman's knee.

How wood rots against the tide
good for hunting grub.
How to fade and fall back into the wind.

He translated her pulse
into near-language. Their poetry so personal
even Peterson's Field Guide could not tap it.

Only a stray hunter saw it.
Shook his head once thinking it a trick
of wind and wing then turned his eyes north

to search for the simple flight
of Brant or Canadian. Those patterns
he could easily understand.

That last night they drank from the river.
Sucked its delicate cusps of mold
sang anti-social songs as if they were humans.

When he flicked his handsome head
to catch the drift of wind
she even managed a single tear.

She waited through days and nights
of grief. Circled the city less
then settled on the wires.

The metallic conductor captured her eyes.
She remembered how he proudly sang her name
as he pranced from pole-top to KV line

One last fluff of feathers. One sigh
for all the unnested summers.
One single scratch

one electrical surge of power of love
Then she fell smiling.
A trick he had taught her.

Breaking the Kula Ring

> The Kula ring is a form of ceremonial
> trade used in the Trobriand Islands of
> New Guinea to establish intertribal
> relationships that last for years.

I am leaving the house
outside the landlord energetically
scrapes away old paint
I have passed a year
shedding a dozen neuroses
have been irritated by noise
food, the dull repetition of breathing
I have traded months of silence
with this house
the months like so many shells
of love and hate binding me to bargains
I can not keep
now the cycle ends
the hours move counterclockwise
each month a precious circle of days
each day a fragile bead

the landlord has waited
through weeks of sunshine
it is cloudy today
and he paints frantically
slaps on coats of color
as bland as his urban mood
I have packed old clothes
tissue padded Xmas gifts
and stored away sad songs
like the one my daughter sings
of lost husbands and stray sons
her voice plaintive as a broken reed
wistful as the bent flowers
which the landlord has now decked
with drops of chemically sweet paint

he waves as we fall into pattern
behind the moving van
I think he is happy
his hand signals a cheerful goodbye
though I cannot see his smile
I turn away from his paint flecked
ladder, away from the house
from the memories of laughter
and dreams, the unfinished metaphors
now trapped in hollow rooms
it is over, closed
like all the windows
the landlord has painted shut

Waiting for Reasons

you fly through a winter
heavy with death and snow
the death of friends
                    dogs
                    us
crystalline branches of cold
definite and long
crisp and beautifully coated
blending into your grey mood
like colors of the silver fox
running silently along snow lines
                    of tundra

you are no newcomer to this
no summer cheechako
you remember another winter
                    another wife
you watch your friends
fly into fog
lose the feel of fixed wing
and plow into horizons
empty as dead end streets
                    or our hearts

You watch us in the mirror
                    of old photos
cheerfully profiled together
now we are lost in the scenery
two icebergs like twins
                    of Lazarus
or oddly matched socks

we are lost among
                    unsigned letters
growing mean as grounded eagles
and children are confused
in the face of it

There Are No Absolutes

Vernella Paige sat in the room
above the tavern waiting
for her lover
The flower dress ladies
sat on back porches
sucking their teeth
She's gone to ruin
pining over that man they said
I never understood it then
never understood how her cat
grey eyes could grow dull
over some dark brown two legged
creature moody as the edge of night
the way her man had been
We kids knew, sure as anything
Vernella could walk
the tops of picket fences
without a scratch
could howl at the moon in her near
whisky voice and sashay through
the humid staccato rhythms
of St. Louis summer nights
brazen as you please
Besides, what man in his right mind
would not want to hold
that lemon yellow cat eyed body

Gone to ruin they said
spreading their bread dough hips
while Vernella sat waiting
for her lover's ghost to untie
the noose from the beam
above the bar and pour
her yet another shot
I never understood why she waited
until that summer when I swallowed
my own lonely days
and waited for my lover
to rise from his bottle of pills
To hold me once again
and let my fingers trace
the strong slant of his nose
where it flared into nostrils
fanning like black velvet wings
Time is scaly as a forty pound cactus
or endless as a frozen scream
a collection of yesterdays
a space created by our own fingers
We are what the earth tells us
we are what we have always been
you and I and the flower dress women

A Poem For My Old Age

I have made my grandmotherly hat
a tiny black one
        with a single flower
I have saved an umbrella
        black and sturdy
and found a cottage to house
my black bones
a little place
        over the freeway
        under the bridge
where my grandchildren will come
        singing
doubtful as any generation
of the young
I will tell them stories
tell them
        take off your glasses
your three dimensional rose colored
        glasses
the world is full of enchanted frogs
remove one lens
        they croak
remove the other
        they beg to be kissed
they are everywhere
        terra cotta and ceramic frogs
frogs sitting inside glass slippers
        the white house
        the rotunda
frogs passing as fertility gods
frogs with crew cuts for summer
a whole congress of frogs
        as mummified as Osiris

frogs under Mickey Mouse hats
                with Cheshire grins
frogs with frizzy hair and tribal names
frogs with enormous tits and blonde wigs
frogs with carrots growing out of their ears
                sitting   singing
through the trees
down by the river
                in buildings   and shopping centers
my children will cluck their tongues
their children will tousle my hair
they will leave
bells tinkling   motors humming
                over the freeway
                under the bridge
                        singing in the gathering dusk
grandma   grandma
                shaking their heads
not hearing the croaks
as they pass
                the nodding toadstools

IV

Defining It For Vanessa

She is too young to eat
chocolates
they blossom on her black face
like peppercorns
she is 16 and dreams
of the alphabet stitched
to the winter wool
of teenage gladiators
in single capital letters
she leans across the table
and asks us older ladies
about love and the future
but we cannot see past
a few days at any time
we are pregnant
with memories
and move slowly
like Egyptian geese grazing

we tell her put Xmas
in your eyes
and keep your voice low
knowing this answer
as insane as any
will soothe her
while she dreams
wrapped like a mummy
inside her flowered sheets
she thinks we hold secrets
and watches us closely
as we shop for dried flowers
lovely center pieces
for the best china
we tell her smiling

later when we describe
our little aches and pains
she turns away
puzzled by antidotes
of blues reds and greens
we tell her how the reds
stick like anger
or clock the tides of the moon
we tell her how she'll guard
her lovely eyes
how only in her blackness
will she grow
large as the moon
we tell how women
with whiskey voices
will try to stop her
how men will strip her clean
of secrets
how the flesh hurts
how the world does not end
with the body
but the longing for it

How to Become a Mistress

First there is the caution
The circled questions
And wine to sweeten the answers
You take note of body lines
The angle of neck that you like
The blunt fingers or slant of mouth
That leave you uncertain
You circle, both closing
And widening the distance between you
There is the touch
Feather light and accidental
You sharpen your eyes
Matching look for look
Touch again, this time
Firm but quick
Another glass of wine, another look
And the answer is sweeter
You take care to undress
With fluid motions
Making certain no sudden movements
Will break the encircled arms
The clenched lips
You check your greed
Holding back, performing
On a lonely stage for an empty house
You test your skills, teasing pleasure
You are waiting for the warming shock
The new feeling of strangeness
For the one second of closing
This world outside your universe
You trap the world
In a warm wet circle between you
Then awake, cautious

Conjure Poem

waiting, wanting
to bring you to me
I call you
in a song full of questions
and melodies of dark answers
I pull you from uncertainty
and wait to soothe you
with sweet scents, olives
plums and silks

wanting to bring you to me
I knit a single chain
of fine wool
to bind your tight muscles
I will unravel it
in blinding light
waiting as you twirl into my arms
dizzily maddened
by my special yarn
and clicking black needles

I will linger in your hair
finger-comb your mustache
and lure the cold spots
from your eyes
I will write poems
on your shoulders
letting the stanzas
drift towards morning

Wild Gardens

you asked
about lovers
yes
I've looked for one
tried several
the first one pinched
my big toe
and muttered in Slavic
his coming too easy
friends later told me
he said
"dandelions, pansies
petunias"
too much
even in Slavic
the second was full
of intrigue
he changed cars
the meeting place
the time
smiled from the left
side only
and never answered
to his real name
I was too confused
to find him
in the end
oh, but I loved
his pale grey trench coat
white carnations and copper skin
the next fellow
I'd rather not discuss
saw him only once
said he couldn't understand
gladiolas
and wore socks
always

the short one was best
no taller than my knees
but quite handy with ladders
he'd lick his way
to my lips
arrive salty and ecstatic
poor dear fell
broke his hip trying to erase
a circle of mustard
from the mole
of my left breast
don't laugh
it was no bed of roses
none of them were demanding
they left me happy
and always took great care
to remove the tears
collected
when I thought of you

The Silence

my head face down in the pillow
your arms brushing against crisp sheets

your breath filtered through
elongated puffs of smoke

sacred as a cat's breath in a dark room
swift as pigeon's wings in city fog

the stillness of my waiting,
the squeak of eyelids, closing   closing

my body ringed
in its own definite space

small sounds snap into
the tight fist of your belly

your body warming all the air
in the hollows around me

a knee moving to the sound
of brushed cotton, slowly   slowly

the vastness of space
when you move away

and I, never so lonely
as when you are near me

SHAZAM

you are like a radio show
all sound effects and no visuals

I use my imagination
to think of love
and you

I am swallowed by staged associations
the fake backdrops and intimate talks

my head is full
of crazy love songs
heavy with violins
and poignant sunsets

pillows fall heavy as bodies
my heart gallops like a broken clock

I have come to believe
my screams are not real
but the squeal of feathers
jerked from the fat bodies
of snowy owls

I manufacture our love scenes
imagine I'm trapped in the eye of a blizzard
and you are the great bearded Mountie

when you touch me
I collapse
upon your manly scent
and once again
the world is saved

meanwhile back at the ranch
there is the real you

stumbling and staggering
through our failure
looking for a villain

you shuffle the dialog faster than a magician
I'm never sure who I'm kissing

should I remember
the heroine's lines
popcorn and Clark Kent

when I see a 1930's film I remember Saturday
matinees, papa's cigars, saltwater dumplings

but when I remember you
I laugh for Godzilla
king of all the beasts

To My Audience

Don't touch me
unless you want me.
The muffled shape
that you hide in
leaves my thighs longing
for more words.
My bed is lonely,
but full of dreams
where I am cushioned
inside your soft laughter.
You are a master of disguises.
When I reach out,
sensuous,
you stand behind a child's mask,
tease me like any brat.
I know your kisses
will be sticky.
I know you will claim me
as trophy,
taken by your slingshot
singly aimed and blue to the mark
like the smugness in your eyes.
You could be father, brother
and give me courage,
but you run through the neighborhood
laughing at my mistakes.
Even you are my error,
round, firm or soft,
medieval or modern,
I never know.
When I drop my head to your chest,
you never stroke my sentences
into rhythms.
You force me into strange characters.
I cannot control the scenes,
the dialogue escapes me,
I seep through holes
in my own paragraphs.

To Whom Do You Wish To Speak

on the hour I begin
I am eight years old
thin as a spider
my dress is seersucker
I still hate it
he nods urging me on
lacing and unlacing his fingers
in excting pyramids
I have an old tennis ball
no net no court no partner
I am black and lonely
the game is Irish
I play for hours counting O'Leary's
against the dull brick wall
the ball bounces rhythmically
to my tune
first the wall my hip my arm
a child's practice
for womanly gestures
he nods again
he has been trained to wait
to watch as I rush frantically
from one year to the next
in this black shroud of skin
I change and change again
looking for the me that is me
he says I must open doors
I tell him a husband story
a farm where cow tits
are colder than ice cubes
and love is the hay mow
the wood stove
and dad's sweaty overalls
he is not convinced
he wants to walk through my memories
but I am lost and do not know the way

I stumble through the past
where images squirm like maggots
sightless mindless bodies
white and writhing in the muck
Victorian nightmares
as detailed as Brueghel paintings
or modern as Bearden collages
better yet
childlike and full of bright doom
but he is not repulsed
he asks for this
he wants to know the I that is she

forty-three minutes remain
sixty second punctuations click
mid-story or silence
as the clock dumbly flicks
through another hour
I am walking home from school
the rag man smiles at me
he picks his way through trash
piled in dark corners of the alley
I follow his ugly back as he stumbles
past the crumpled bricks
I am ten and rubbish fascinates me
I give him a penny for the old garden basket
hanging from a nail of his pushcart
the wind is still nothing moves
I have yet to feel the bigot's cold cheek
but this man is black
and I know what he knows
I do not cry when his yellow teeth
bruise purple upon my lips
in the silence a little girl skips away
I become what I am
I am what I watch

now I ask if duality is the game of success
who can say what we are he frowns
this is she it is I
we are pronouns abandoned
by all nouns
I am the crazy lady escaping
from Sexton's poems
my house is on fire my children are gone
I am the lady in the bank without a check
the poet who forgot her lines
by day I sing in the first row
of the Church of Our Name in Christ choir
my flowered hat askew
above my black powdered face
I need no degrees for this
by night I ring the bells in Bedlam
I have no name
I am the forty-three year old masturbator
friendless and lonely
inside the poetry of Ai's *Cruelty*
grateful for the small taste of anything

he waits as I untangle a thread of words
I have sewn myself inside a web of rules
he promises nothing
like any good doctor he offers no omens
Thou shall not this
Thou shall not that
are reserved for mothers and priests
be patient he quotes
knowing I am the patient
the chameleon chasing myself
like the frilled gecko
I am the lizard who will not cast a shadow
wizened and tattered I slide among books
in search of honest secrets
a woman of letters
licking each metaphor clean
I supplement this diet
with the comfort of black earth
the coolness of black skin

I fumble and start again
tell him the one about dreams
there is a cave
the sun is a single eye
there are owls in the trees
they have ears
the bushes bear no fruit
I am twelve then twenty
now I have a lover now I don't
you touch me here
I touch you there
the world is white and electric
suddenly it is not
is that all he smiles
I answer him from still another face
there is no end, lies are truth
my life is without corners
we will move round and round
never closing the circles